William Bolcom

Lilith

for E-flat Alto Saxophone and Piano

Commissioned by the National Endowment for the Arts for the Saxophone and Piano duos:
Donald Sinta & Ellen Weckler; Joseph Wytko & Walter Cosand; Laura Hunter & Brian Connelly

ISBN 978-0-634-07302-1

EDWARD B. MARKS MUSIC COMPANY

EXCLUSIVELY DISTRIBUTED BY
HAL•LEONARD®
7777 W. BLUEMOUND RD. P.O. BOX 13819 MILWAUKEE, WI 53213

COMPOSER'S NOTE:

LILITH: A female demon believed to haunt desolate places. She is
identified in a Canaanite charm of the eighth century B.C., and likewise in
post-Biblical Jewish literature, with the child-stealing witch of worldwide
folklore. The name derives from Sumerian "lil," "wind" (i.e. "spirit")...

Lilith (לילית; LXX ὀνοκἐυταυρος; Vulg. *Lamia*. "the night hag"; Isaiah
34:14). Lilith is the Akkadian *lilitu*, female counterpart of a demon called
lilú. In Mesopotamian texts she appears primarily as the *succuba*, who
tempts men in sexual dreams... She is depicted by Isaiah as haunting
desolate places in company with such unclean birds as the kite, pelican,
and owl and with such ghoulish beasts as wildcats and jackals. [She is
found in European folklore and ancient Roman literature; also in
Aristophanes and ancient Akkadian and Jewish texts.] ... In ancient Greece
the child-stealing witch was sometimes known as Mormolukeion --
i.e. "Bogey-wolf" (Aristophanes *Thesmophoriazusa*; Plato *Phaedo*).

--from Biblical dictionaries

Isaiah 34:14: Wild cats will meet hyenas there
the satyrs will call to each other
there too will Lilith take cover
seeking rest.

--The Jerusalem Bible

PERFORMANCE NOTES:

- The E♭ Alto Saxophone part in the score sounds a major 6th lower than written.

- Accidentals remain in force within beamed groups except where otherwise marked.

- All signs and special notation are explained in the body of the musical text, except:

= pauses, from long to short in duration (5" → 1/4")

for Laura Hunter and Brian Connelly

Lilith
I. The Female Demon

Duration: 13:00

WILLIAM BOLCOM
(1984)

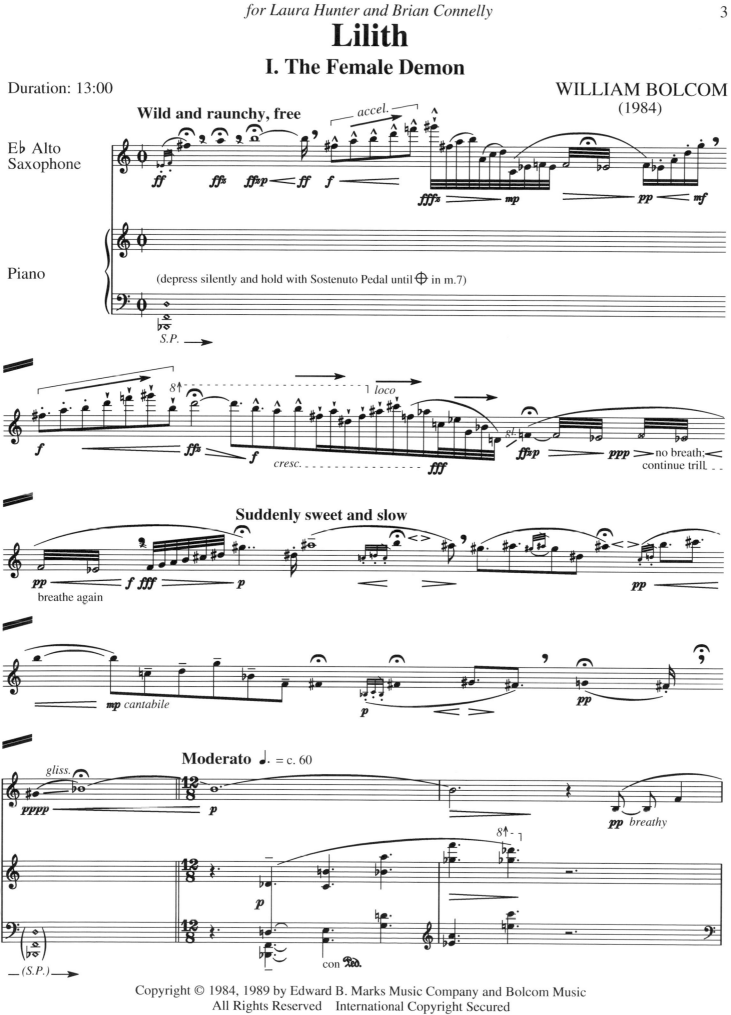

✦ ⬆ and ⬇ = highest- and lowest-notes clusters (chromatic)

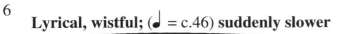

Lyrical, wistful; (♩ = c.46) suddenly slower

⊛ ▮ = multiphonic smack sound   ⊛⊛ like the cry of a roc!

Apr. 2, 1984 Ann Arbor

II. Succuba

Adagio religioso

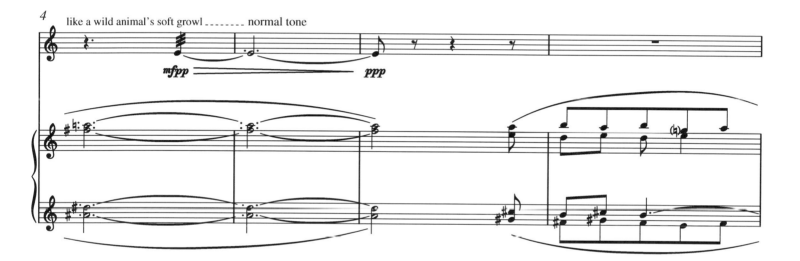

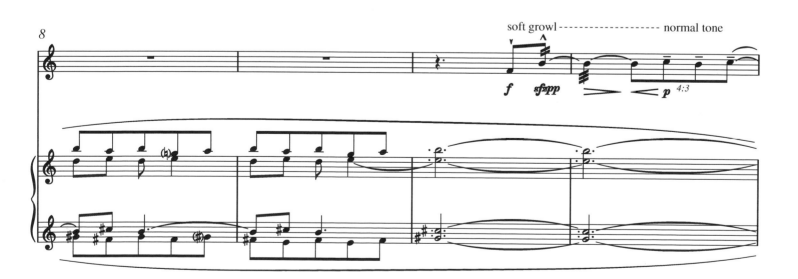

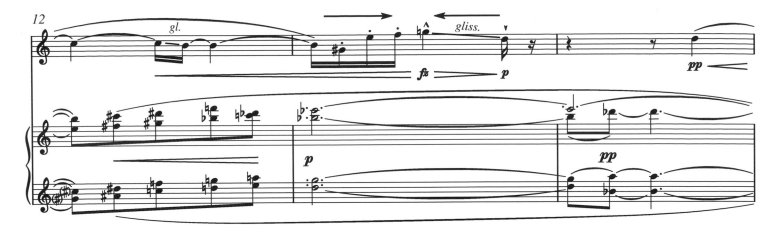

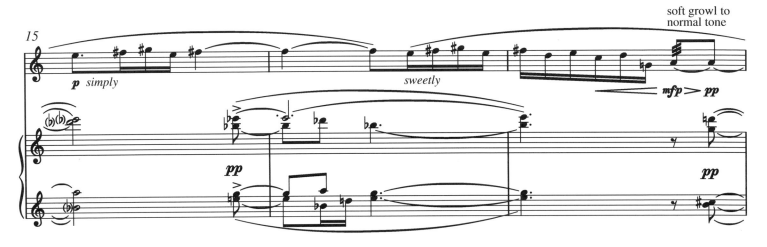

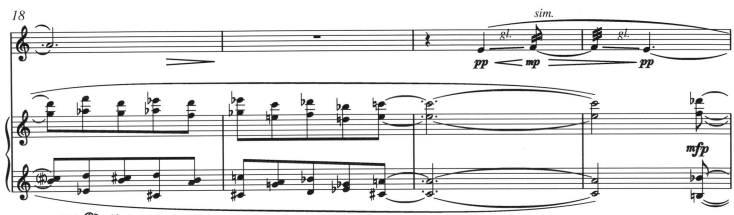

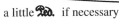

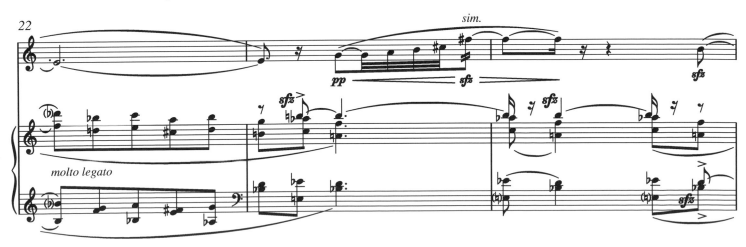

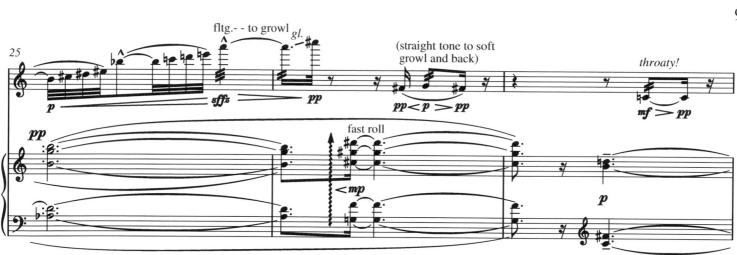

poco agitato

A tempo

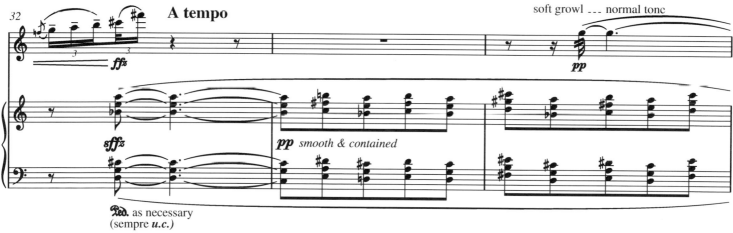

May 14, 1984 New York City

III. Will-o'-the-Wisp

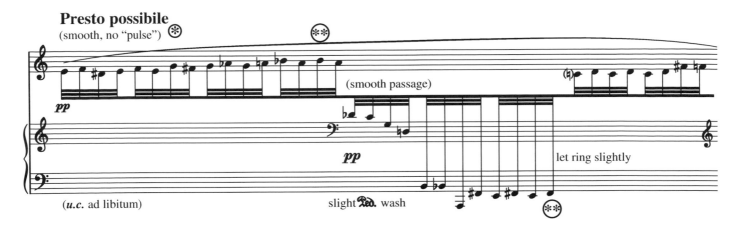

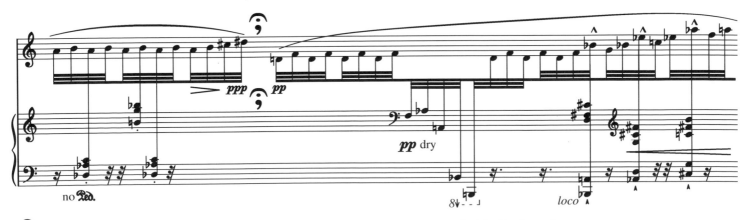

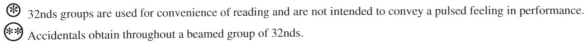

✳ 32nds groups are used for convenience of reading and are not intended to convey a pulsed feeling in performance.

✳✳ Accidentals obtain throughout a beamed group of 32nds.

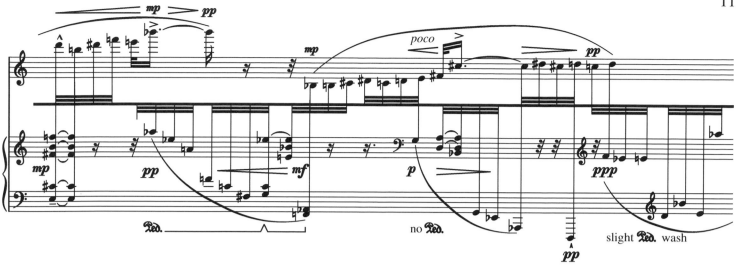

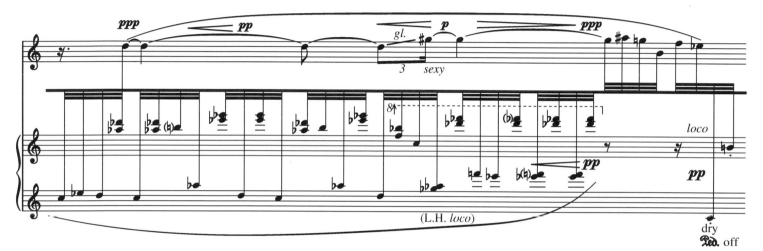

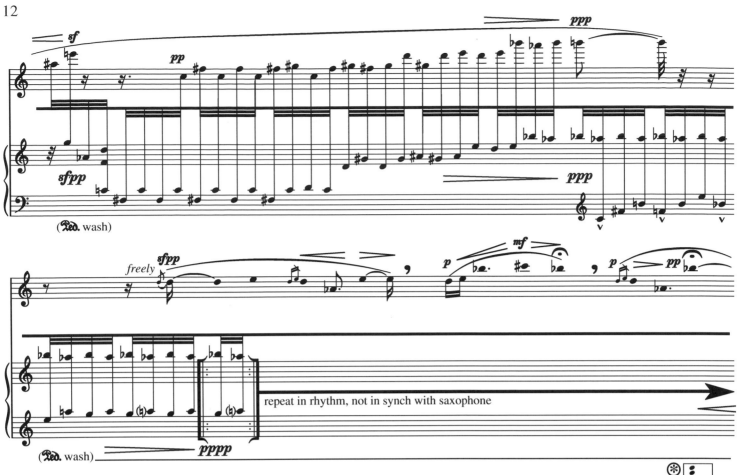

repeat in rhythm, not in synch with saxophone

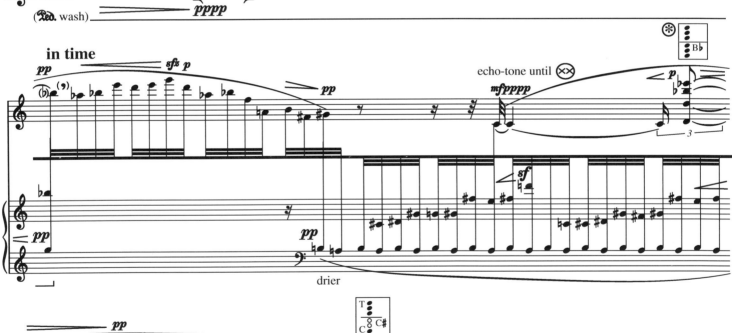

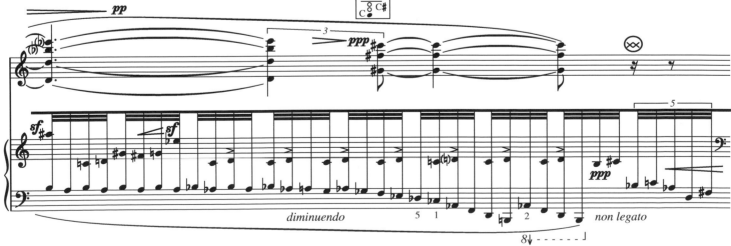

✳ Fingerings according to R. Caravan

for Laura Hunter and Brian Connelly

Lilith

I. The Female Demon

Eb ALTO SAXOPHONE

WILLIAM BOLCOM
(1984)

II. Succuba

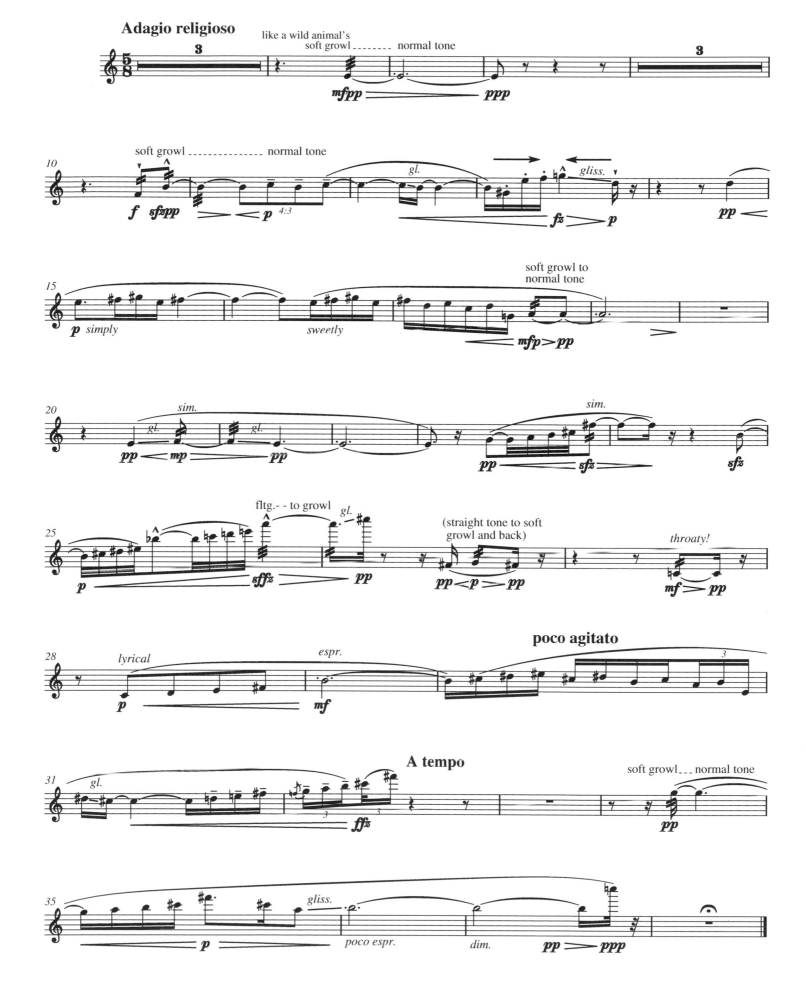

III. Will-o'-the-Wisp

Presto possibile
(smooth, no "pulse") ✸   ✸✸

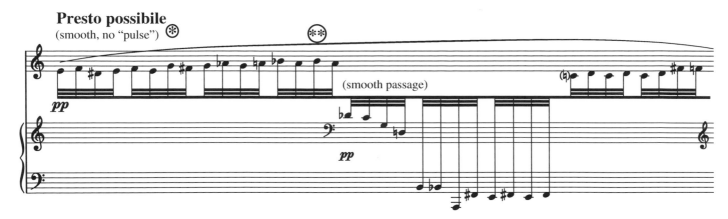

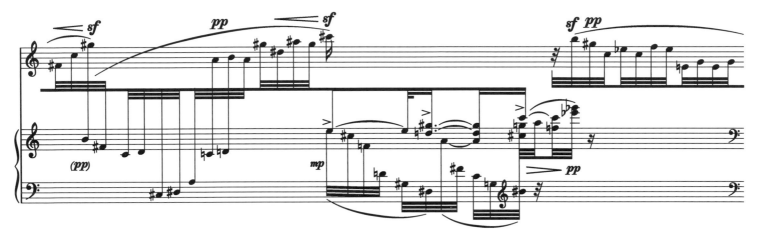

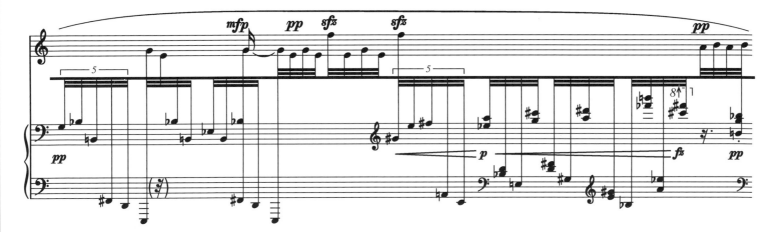

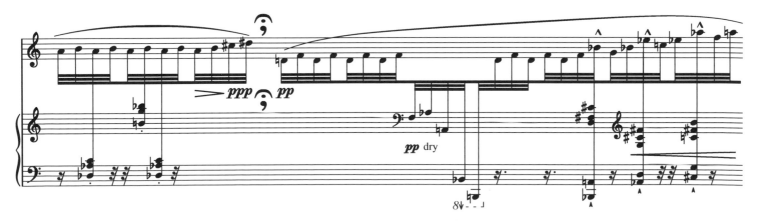

✸ 32nds groups are used for convenience of reading and are not intended to convey a pulsed feeling in performance.

✸✸ Accidentals obtain throughout a beamed group of 32nds.

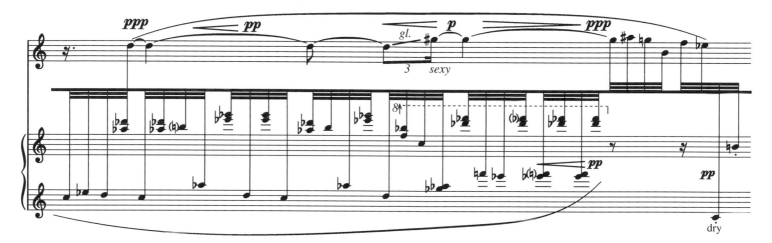

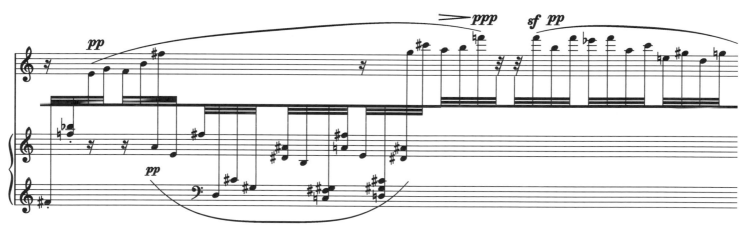

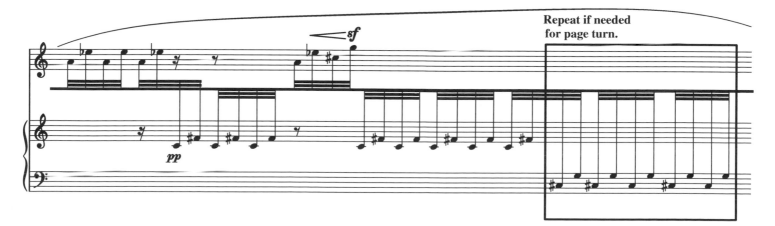

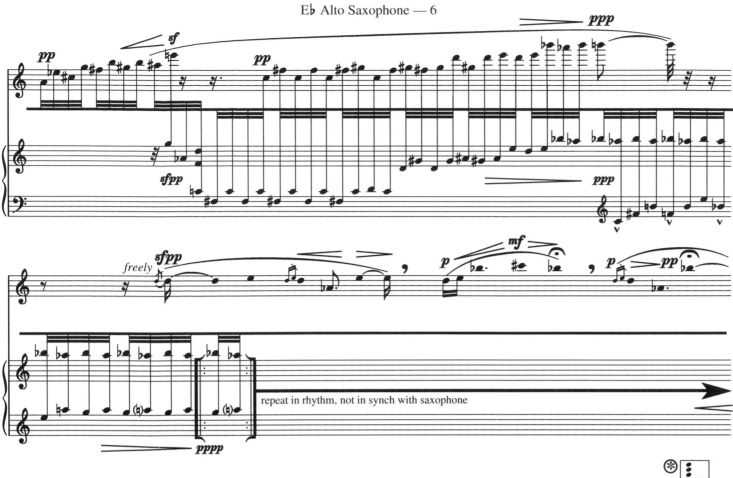

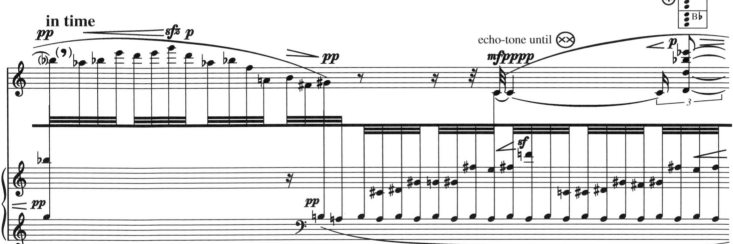

repeat in rhythm, not in synch with saxophone

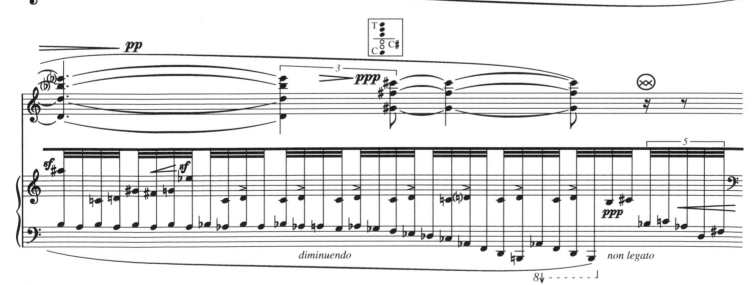

echo-tone until ⊗

diminuendo

non legato

⊛ Fingerings according to R. Caravan

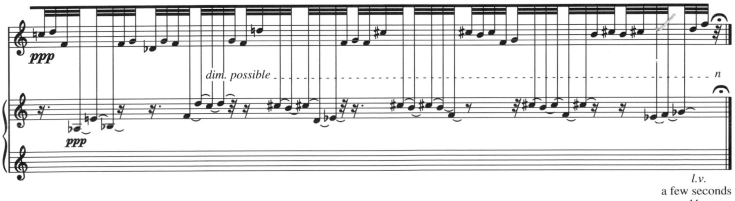

IV. Child-Stealer

V. The Night Dance

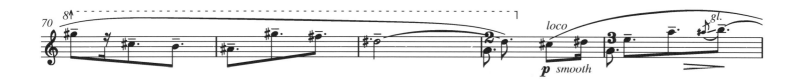

✳ a very short fermata, if at all.

✳✳ or similar grotesque multiphonics to (m. 57).

attacca
Saarbrücken – Ann Arbor
June 18, 1984

IV. Child-Stealer

Free, slow

Sax: play into piano throughout movement (but see final note).

✹ 〰〰〵 = unpitched <u>slide</u> up to note

✹✹ If struts inside piano interfere with chords, redispose (by octave displacement) any or all chord pitches until conveniently placed.

June 29, 1984 Ann Arbor

V. The Night Dance

Easy at first

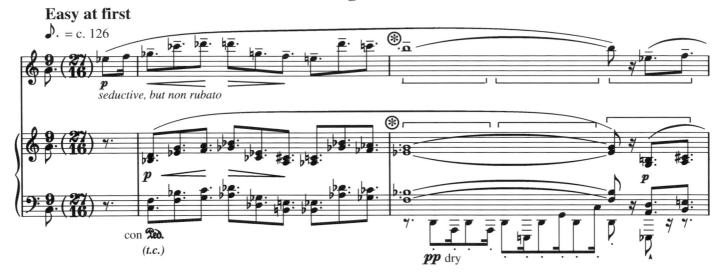

seductive, but non rubato

con Ped.
(t.c.)

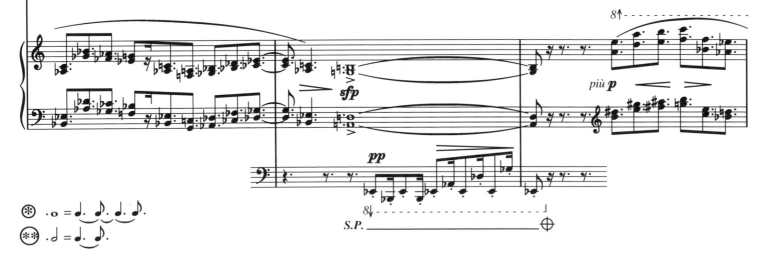

S.P.

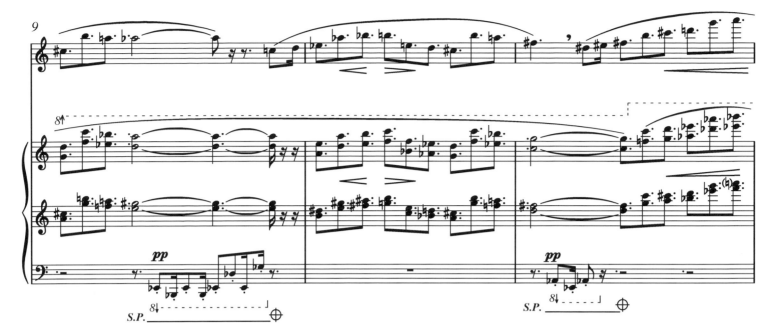

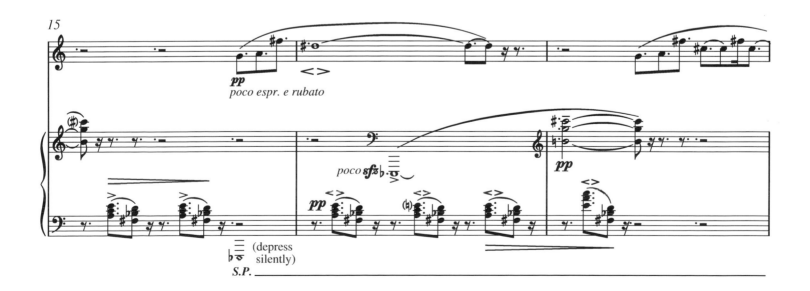

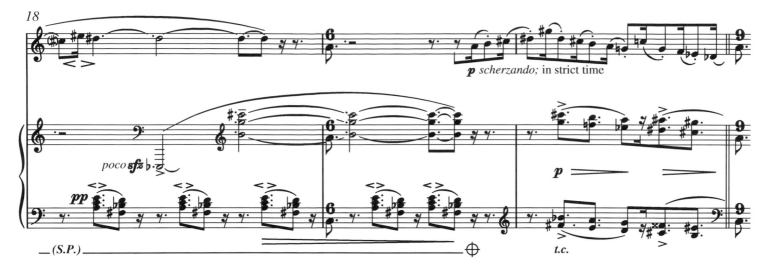

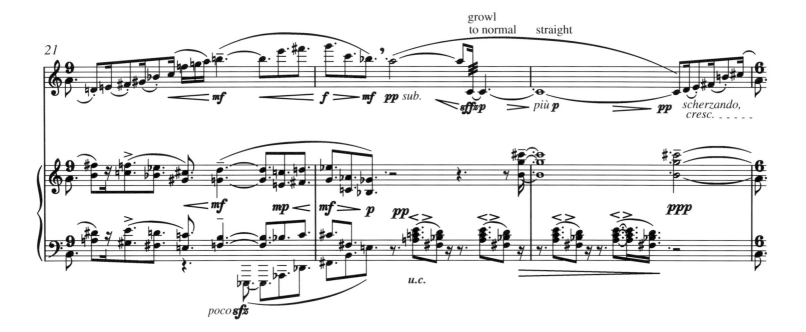

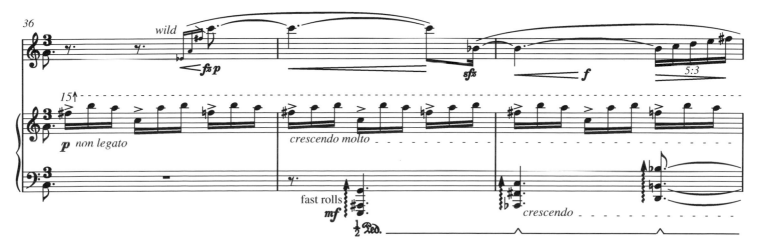

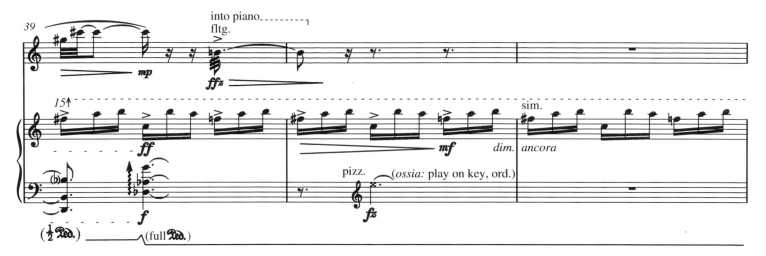

⊛ a very short fermata, if at all.

⊛⊛ or similar grotesque multiphonics (to m. 57)

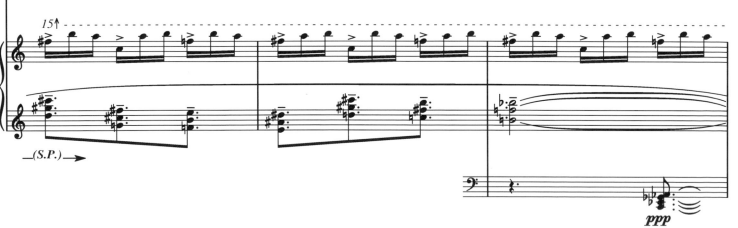

June 28, 1984 Ann Arbor